Quic

Emotional Intelligence

C000179326

The small changes that make a big difference

Quick Fix Your Emotional Intelligence

Dr Harry Alder

How To Books

Published by How To Books Ltd,
3 Newtec Place, Magdalen Road,
Oxford OX4 1RE. United Kingdom.
Tel: (01865) 793806. Fax: (01865) 248780.
email: info@howtobooks.co.uk
http://www.howtobooks.co.uk

British Library Cataloguing in Publication Data.

A catalogue record for this book is available from the British
Library.

Cover design by Shireen Nathoo Design, London
Cover illustration by Roger Langridge
Cartoons by Grizelda Grizlingham

Produced for How To Books by Deer Park Productions
Design and Typeset by Shireen Nathoo Design, London
Printed and bound in Great Britain

NOTE: The material contained in this book is set out in good faith
for general guidance and no liability can be accepted for loss or
expense incurred as a result of relying in particular circumstances
on statements made in the book. Laws and regulations are
complex and liable to change, and readers should check the
current position with the relevant authorities before making
personal arrangements.

Contents

About the Author

Dr Harry Alder is an international management seminar presenter and prolific author. A businessman with vast experience of senior positions in major companies, he is a popular keynote conference speaker and consultant. His many books, covering management development, leadership, creativity and NLP, and translated into a score of languages, have gained a growing global audience.

Preface

IQ (intelligence quotient) has gained much credence over the years and is now well embedded in our western educational tradition. That's fine – as far as it goes. But it doesn't go far. In fact IQ is more at home in the classroom and the academic and scientific worlds in which verbal, numerical skills are particularly valued. In the world most of us know, you need other kinds of resourcefulness, and in particular 'people skills' to succeed in life

That's where EQ – *emotional* intelligence (sometimes referred to as emotional quotient) comes in. This is the *emotional* equivalent of cognitive IQ. EQ has caught the popular imagination. It embraces two aspects of 'intelligence'.

1   Understanding yourself, your goals and intentions, emotions and all.

2   Second, understanding others, and their feelings.

Not surprisingly, the ability to manage your emotions appropriately, whilst showing empathy and relating well to others, is a better predictor of success than the kind of abstract intelligence measured by IQ.

Two Americans, Peter Salovey (Yale) and John Mayer (New Hampshire) coined the term emotional intelligence. It was later popularised by Daniel Goleman in his book *Emotional Intellingence*. Five 'domains' were identified.

* knowing your emotions

* managing your emotions

* motivating yourself

* recognising emotion in others

* handling relationships.

These are essentially the 'people skills', or 'social competencies' that tend to have the biggest effect on our everyday lives. They have repeatedly been shown to correlate to 'doing well in life' or 'success' as most people define it, regardless of educational attainments and IQ score.

The good news is that anyone can increase their EQ and enjoy the benefits immediately in their life. We are conditioned by 'left brain' education. In institutions and organisations, IQ reigns. But we can each reclaim our innate intelligence as a person and experience the benefits – however belatedly.

By following the simple principles and guidelines in this book you will get to know yourself better, be sure about what you really want, and 'discover' what is important to you. You will learn to manage your emotions as *resources* and incorporate them into *better quality thinking*. You will communicate and relate better with others. And new achievement of all kinds will follow.

You can translate this self-knowledge and influencing skills into achieving your own, worthwhile purposes. The changes will affect your whole life. And they will start immediately. You just need to *know* and *do* the key things that will quick fix your emotional intelligence. And you will learn how to do that in this little book.

Harry Alder

Chapter One

Know What You Want

True intelligence operates for a purpose.
*It has meaning. It **gives** meaning. So you*
need to know your purposes. What you want
to achieve. What you want to be.

IQ – the traditional measure of
intelligence – doesn't tell us who will
reach the top and get the medals. Or who
will make a mark on history, be valued in
their community or live a satisfying life. It
doesn't tell us who will keep going when
others give up. Who will stay motivated
when they only have their own, inner
resources to draw upon. Or who are the

special few that will translate dreams into
reality. This requires emotional
intelligence – EQ.

Emotionally intelligent people have
purpose in their lives. They have self-
knowledge – sometimes called
intrapersonal (intra = within) intelligence.
But even the most goal-oriented person
may need to step back from time to time
and identify what motivates them, what is
important to them, and what might be
going on underneath the surface of a busy
life. We can all boost our EQ and start
living and achieving with a purpose.

MAKING YOUR WANTS LIST

First, think about what you want then
write out a list. What you want might be
what you want to:

* get or have

* do

* know

* be.

Writing out a list is not just a memory
jogger or checklist. It is an important stage
in sorting out your priorities. Try to
express your goals as they occur to you,
and in the words that come to your mind:

* 'I would like to. . . '

* 'I wish I. . . '

And so on.

First, you'll need to reflect on what you want and then express your desires clearly. This is an important part of self-knowledge and EQ. So don't skip it. You will be using this self-information later.

Your initial list should:

* be as long as you like

* include both short-term and long-term goals

* include wishes as well as definite objectives

* be done quickly and intuitively.

This process can be enjoyable and therapeutic. It is one of the foundations of self-knowledge and a lot of what you do and achieve will depend on doing it thoroughly.

FILTERING YOUR GOALS

Making a 'wants list' is a straightforward
exercise anyone can do. The 'intelligent'
part comes next. You now need to filter
your wants and wishes in such a way that
you finish up doing what you really want.
In this chapter you will learn how to set
and attain *quality* goals that are worth
achieving. And, more importantly, how to
set goals that have a good chance of
success.

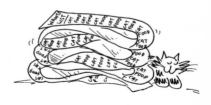

EQ GOAL-TESTING QUESTIONS

Ask yourself the following questions in relation to each of your goals.

Is my Goal Clear, Specific and Unambiguous?

The less specific your goal, the easier it is to make excuses if you don't achieve it. That's an all too common cause of non-achievement. That's why it helps to write it out clearly. However, your goal is more than a written-down intention. It's something inside you that motivates you and unconsciously directs you towards it – like a missile aims towards its programmed target. So you need to be clear and specific in your own mind about what you are setting out to achieve.

There are many ways to make a goal more specific. For example:

*   You can put a measurement on it: 'I want to be 9 stone'; 'I want £20,000 a year'.

*   You can put a date on it: ' . . .within six months', or 'by the end of the year'.

*   You can be very precise about your goal: 'I want to get a B in French'.

*   You can set out the stages you will need to reach, or break your goal into

parts ('I need to do so and so, then so and so, then . . .').

The 'specific' goal principle is simple:

....

Don't kid yourself. By being specific, you will know if and when you achieve your goal and you will know just as surely if you don't.

....

That's the intelligent approach to getting what you want.

Is My Goal within My Personal Control?

There are plenty of worthwhile goals concerning your family, employer, community and the wider world, which are not within your personal control. You simply don't have enough influence or resources to make them happen. No matter how determined you are, you have little chance of fulfilling goals that depend upon other people. It makes more EQ sense to spend your time more effectively on things you can achieve yourself, and take personal responsibility for.

Ask these sorts of questions:

* What can I do, personally, to bring about this goal?

* Who am I dependent upon to achieve it?

* What if so-and-so doesn't do his or her part?

Identify the part you can do something about, even if it is indirect. You will then have some *influence* over your goal and your future.

As it happens, by doing your own tasks well you will help towards achieving another's goals anyway. For instance, what your employer, partner or your child wants. You may decide to spend 'quality time' with your children, for instance, or to contribute financially to their education or career. Decide what you can do to support them in *their* goals, which only they can take responsibility for.

This principle is similar to the 'specific, unambiguous' test:

···

The fewer people you can blame for non-performance the better.

···

Is My Goal at the Right Level?

Don't aim so high that you don't know where to start, you mentally 'blank off', and can hardly imagine succeeding. On the other hand, don't aim so low that you will not have the motivation or challenge to get started, and – often more importantly – to keep going. If achieving a goal does not have its own *inbuilt sense of satisfaction*, it is probably at the wrong level.

This doesn't necessarily mean you have to delete the goal from your list, but you may have to amend or adapt it. For instance, a big or complex task can be broken into smaller, more manageable chunks. Alternatively, by giving yourself a tighter deadline you can make a less demanding job more challenging and motivating.

Is My Goal Positive?

Given a free hand at saying what they want, many people are surer about what they *don't* want. For instance:

* 'I certainly don't want a manager's job after what Viv went through.'

* 'I wouldn't want to move away from the family.'

* 'I've no longer got any sporting ambitions.'

And so on.

The 'positive' goal principle is not just about 'positive thinking'. The human mind works towards achieving clearly visualised, 'internalised' goals. It doesn't seem to handle a negative as a negative. Thus, if you dwell on what you *don't* want, there is an extraordinary tendency for it to be self-fulfilling. Put another way:

....

You will get what you think about most.

....

We experience this strange phenomenon all the time. Told 'you mustn't spill it' or 'you've got to avoid the bunker on the left' or 'you must keep off the chocolates', we tend to do just what we tried to avoid – spilling it, landing in the bunker, and eating the forbidden chocolates. Making your goals positive is an easy, quick fix that can turn round your life. Here's the simple rule:

....

*Imagine what you **want** rather than what you **don't** want.*

....

To start with, you can change the *language* of each goal on your list. Usually a simple reversal is enough. If not, ask yourself,

* 'If I don't want that, then what *do* I want?'

Write it down in new, positive language. Which is the better goal according to this principle?

* To 'lose half a stone' (negative), or

* to 'reach 9 stone by Christmas' (positive)?

You've got it! This simple device will make your goals clear, positive and more achievable.

How Will I Know When I Have Achieved My Goal?

If you have done a good job on the goal tests so far, this one will be easy and enjoyable. It concerns expressing your goal in *sensory* language and imagery. Think about what you want in sights, sounds and feelings. Ask:

* What will I look like?

* What will I feel like?

* What will they say?

* What will I see?

* What other sounds will there be?

* What else will I notice about my goal
   as it happens?

The mental trick is to imagine – to
experience – having fully achieved your
goal. This *internalises* your goal in a much
stronger way than a written statement or a
repeated 'affirmation'. It reflects the way
your mind works, and the real world that
(to you) is just such a collection of
sensory experience.

There are quick fix ways to develop this
crucial imagining skill. Take one of your
top few goals and try experiencing each
'modality' – sights, sounds, feelings –
separately. Then combine them, and notice
how they seem more realistic. They now

provide a clear, multi-sensory internal
target – the sort of intelligent goal you are
more likely to achieve.

Have I Got What it Takes to Achieve My Goal?

The question 'have I got what it takes?' applies to what you are capable of *now*. It's not a matter of genes or educational advantage. You need not be limited by lack of skill if you can *acquire* those skills, or lack of knowledge if you can *acquire* that knowledge. These are just *extra goals* to which all the rules in this chapter apply.

We mostly underestimate what we are capable of achieving. In fact, this question usually applies only to the most fundamental of human resources such as age and physical build.

Thus, if a goal 'takes' youth, and you don't have youth, then you may not have 'what it takes'. If it takes a big, sturdy build, and you are little and waspish, you may not have 'what it takes'. However, if it takes fitness, and you can *get* fit, then there isn't a problem. Likewise, it may require the kind of skills and dexterity that you can acquire with training and application. Again, no problem, at least on this goal criterion. So answer the question honestly, but:

∗   Don't short-change yourself.

∗   Don't measure yourself against past failures.

* Be prepared to adjust your goal to allow for limitations you can't do much about.

* Consider whether you can *get* what it takes by adding a few challenging goals.

What or Who Else Might be Affected?

Success and failure are usually judged only in a particular context, or from a particular viewpoint. Success for you might mean failure (or at least disappointment) on the part of someone else affected by your 'success'. Similarly, even within your own life, success in your career might not mean success in your family life – and vice versa. Or financial success may not equate to physical health, let alone a sense of fulfilment or 'peace of mind', if those are included in your goals.

Be ready to amend your goals to fit this test and save yourself unnecessary failure.

You may be surprised how a 'downgraded' goal that allows for other people and other compartments of your life gives a greater sense of pleasure and fulfilment.

GOING FOR IT

Intelligent goal setting doesn't happen in a vacuum. Lots of factors may affect whether you achieve what you want, and how you feel upon achieving it. Bring these factors into the equation, sooner rather than later. By applying these simple tests you will know what you want and understand yourself better. That's one of the key characteristics of emotional intelligence that you can fix if you care to.

Chapter Two

Understand Yourself

*In order to know what you want
you also need to know what is
important to you.*

You need to have values. These are
criteria or yardsticks by which you can
measure what is worthwhile and what is
not. Values largely happen at an
unconscious level. But with the know-how
you will gain in this chapter you will soon
discover what is important to you, and be
able to incorporate that self-knowledge
into a more successful life.

What you *want most* will reflect what is
most important to you. The goal list you
prepared in Chapter 1 will probably
reflect those values. At the same time, you
demonstrate your values in the goals you
pursue and the behaviour you adopt to
fulfil them. So values are the other side of
the 'goal coin'.

Values don't appear in the average 'to do'
list, but they have an all-pervading effect
on our lives, affecting everything we say
and do. Identifying your values may not
be as straightforward as making a list of
wants and wishes. However, by asking
yourself the simple questions below, you
will quickly identify what is important
to you.

KNOWING WHAT IS IMPORTANT

A value is what is important to you. If one of your values is honesty, for instance, then honesty is important to you. That means you *believe* in honesty. So your value also forms a *belief*.

'Important' Questions

You can make a quick start by asking:

* 'What is important to me?', or

* 'What are the things I believe in?'

It usually helps to do this for each of the main areas of your life. For instance:

* 'What is most important to me about *my job?*'

* 'What is most important to me about *my family?*'

* 'What is important to me about *my hobbies and interests?*'

* 'What is most important to me about
   my *personal growth and spiritual
   development*?

And so on.

This makes you think honestly about
yourself. In particular, as you reflect on
your values, you will *imagine* yourself
demonstrating them in real life.

Identifying Your Values

You can then identify your values, using
work or career as the first 'testing ground':

Ask: 'What is most important to me about
my job?' For example:

* meeting people?

* using my brain?

* providing for my family?

* using my talents?

Write down your own answers. Then follow up each answer with another question. For example:

* What is important about *meeting people*?

* What is important about *using my brain*?

* What is important about *providing for my family*?

* What is important about *using my talents*?

And so on.

Form your own questions.

Then, using each successive answer, carry on the same process. Ask:

*   'What is important to me about meeting people?'

For example:

*   It makes life interesting.

*   It helps me see other points of view.

*   It can create long-term relationships.

And so on.

Apply this simple process to each part or
'chunk' (work, family, etc) of your life. As
with your goals, as you reflect on your
values a 'pecking order' will emerge. This
is invaluable EQ self-knowledge. When
you face important decisions, or run out
of time, well-thought-out values provide a
personal guide to what should get priority.

As you apply this self-questioning to each area of your life, you may find that you repeat yourself in your answers. This is to be expected. Your basic values apply to different parts of your life and will probably reappear in work, family and social life, and in your personal self-development.

Expect a few inconsistencies also. You may need to re-appraise values that upon reflection are far less important than you had assumed. The good news is that:

···

You are always free to change your values as well as your behaviour.

···

GOING FOR IT

This is an opportunity to increase your 'intrapersonal intelligence' or self-understanding. You will then start to change for the better, and succeed in the things that matter to you most.

Chapter Three

Manage Your Moods

*Emotion is part of what makes
us what we are.*

We all have a rich repertoire of emotional states upon which we can draw, going back to early childhood. This doesn't apply only to emotional people who 'wear their hearts on their sleeves'. We all have feelings. Recent research shows the importance of emotion in what was hitherto considered rational, cognitive thought. Emotion plays an important part in memory, imagination and every 'mental' activity.

Emotional intelligence involves:

* *awareness* – identifying emotional states *as they happen*;

* *understanding* – what emotions are and how they affect us; and

* *control* – using emotions purposely to bring about your goals.

Simply, this aspect of EQ means *thinking about how you feel*. You can be aware of how you feel right now *just by thinking about it*. And it gets quicker and easier with practice.

GETTING INTO A BETTER STATE

Each of the goals you listed in Chapter 1
has an inbuilt emotion. Each goal brings
with it a feeling – of contentment,
pleasure, pride, relief or whatever. That is
the state of mind you *implicitly aimed for*
in setting about your intention. That's
your 'goal state' – the state you want to
get into.

At the same time, you also have a *present*
emotional state, when setting out your
wants and desires. That's the state you are
in prior to a goal being achieved or
behaviour carried out.
It's usually the state
you want to *get out of*.

For instance:

~ *present state: unhappy*
~ desired state: happy

~ *present state: anxious*
~ desired state: calm

~ *present state: ignorant* (of some knowledge)
~ desired state: knowledgeable (in that particular area)

~ *present state: unnoticed*
~ desired state: noticed, respected, valued.

Written-down goals themselves may not
reveal either your present or your desired
state. However, by reflecting and asking
the questions in Chapter 1, you will
usually identify these important aspects of
your wants and wishes. High EQ people
naturally incorporate these *desired states of
mind* into their goals. But anyone can do
that. We can all know, not just *what we
feel*, but also *what we want to feel*, and thus
be more specific in pursuing it.

CHOOSING THE RIGHT EMOTION

There are some emotions that each of us can readily call upon, such as calmness, assertiveness or confidence. These will depend on the sort of person you are – your personality. These are important emotional *resources*, which you can employ to help you achieve your goals, including your desired state, such as happiness.

Emotional intelligence means being able
to *choose* the right emotion for the right
occasion. It means being able to decide
when a particular emotion is appropriate
and when it is not. For instance, when it
would be better to be more angry or less
angry, more calm or less calm.

Ask yourself:

~   'What is the best state to be in to
    achieve my goal?

Harnessing Your Emotional Resources

Such emotional resources are part of *you* and your experience. By recalling a specific memory you will 'replay' the actual emotion of the experience. You have, therefore, a portfolio of emotions you can utilise just by thinking (remembering). Try it. Notice how your pulse rate increases in a moment as you recall an emotionally charged experience.

We tend to undervalue our emotional resources. Some we even consider to be liabilities. However, some emotions, or states of mind, can be more valuable in achieving a goal than other resources, such as time, money or even talent.

So, which emotions do you need to call upon? Simply, whatever emotion is likely to best support and bring about the outcomes you identified in Chapter 1. For instance, if you need to be particularly cool and calm to best fulfil a certain task, then that's the emotional state you want. Used in that way, it is a positive resource – an asset. On the other hand, a situation may call for assertiveness and a certain 'fire in the belly', or a highly psyched up frame of mind.

....

It's emotional horses for emotional courses.

....

Get to know your own emotional
resources and recall them whenever you
need to. Become familiar with being:

*   content

*   happy

*   calm

*   confident

*   satisfied

*   fulfilled

*   exonerated

*   forgiven

* vindicated

* proud

* elated.

And so on.

We have each experienced a bewildering variety of emotions. Any of these might form your 'desired state' – especially the big ones like 'happy' and 'content'. At the same time, any might provide an emotional resource upon which you can call to help you achieve your different goals. For example do you remember a time when someone told you that you'd done a particularly good job, or you felt that you'd completed a task particularly well? How did you feel? I'm sure it raised your level of confidence.

In this way you can call on confidence you have experienced in the past to help you undertake a demanding, new task.

TRY IT NOW

Harnessing your emotional resources is a powerful self-knowledge skill. The following are some ways you can harness 'resident' emotions to help you achieve present goals:

* Imagine how you will feel when you have fully achieved your goal.

* 'Pre-experience' your goal realistically in a multi-sensory way. Carefully notice the sights, sounds and – especially – the feelings of pleasure at success.

* Ask yourself 'When did I feel like that (the resource I now need) at any time

in the past?' Take your time. Allow
your mind to 'freewheel' and your
imagination to engage fully.

* Choose positive, empowering
  memories which you can recall at will.
  You are free to 'tweak' any emotional
  memory to make it more powerful
  and useful.

* Choose memories from different areas
  of your life, not associated with your
  present situation. Optimism in one
  area of your life (such as work), for
  instance, might be invaluable when
  used in another (say your family life).

* Notice the different things that trigger
  these empowering emotions. The

simplest 'input' – a smile, a tune, a mountain view, a brisk winter walk – can produce an abundance of good feelings. These memory 'anchors' are keys to your emotional resources.

Leapfrog 'little' goals

Ask this sort of question:

*   'Is there an easier, quicker, more
    pleasurable way to get the state I
    want?'

You will usually find answers to such
question in your own experience. Ask:

*   'How can I *be* what I want without
    going through the *getting, knowing,* or
    doing?'

Some people are able to find pleasure in each moment, and save themselves a lot of anticlimaxes and the unfulfilment of pursuing shortsighted goals. Aim for the 'being' kind of goals you met in Chapter 1.

Of course, emotions just 'happen'. They are not 'cognitive' thinking. But you can be aware of the process and its effect on you. And even if you can't fathom particular emotions you can learn to use them in a positive way. Intrapersonal intelligence comprises these vital human skills. You don't need a PhD in psychology, let alone a high IQ. The simple principles and techniques you are learning will increase your chances of achieving the 'desired states' in your current list of goals and intentions.

GOING FOR IT

By learning to manage your moods, you will be able to manage your life and achieve what you know you are capable of.

Chapter Four

Understand Others

*By bringing other people into your
goal equation you will understand
them better, and start to realise the
extra benefits of influencing and
communicating effectively.*

One of the goal criteria you met in
Chapter 1 was 'Who or what else
might be affected?' This part of the process
requires *empathy*. Empathy is a major
interpersonal skill and a feature of EQ.
You can develop your empathy rating by
honestly applying this goal criterion to
each goal on your list. Not only will you

be clearer about what you want, but, by taking account of critical 'people factors', you will also increase your chances of achieving your goal.

Being able to understand other people will allow you to realise the extra benefits of influencing and communicating effectively. This is another feature of EQ, and is often termed interpersonal intelligence (inter = among, between). In this chapter you will learn specific ways to understand people better.

SEE FROM DIFFERENT POSITIONS

You need to get the 'perspective' of the other person and be able to see things 'from their point of view'. This is a matter of *perception*, of course. It concerns the *position* from which you view a person, behaviour, circumstance, event or situation. There are three basic 'perceptual positions' which you can adopt in any sort of communication:

1. *First position.* This is your own, subjective perspective. You see things through your own eyes, and feel things that only you can feel. When recalling a memory 'from first

position', you re-experience what you actually experienced. You can likewise imagine yourself in the future from this position.

2. *Second position.* In this position you 'become' the other party in a communication. For instance, if imagining you were being interviewed for a job, you would imagine yourself in the interviewer's place, seeing, hearing and feeling things as they would. If recalling a conversation with a partner or colleague, you would try to see things as if through their eyes, and – especially – feel what they felt.

3. *Third position.* From this position you view things as an outsider, third party observer or 'fly on the wall'. In fact, third perceptual position may take on many specific observer roles. For example, you can take the perspective of:

* a small child

* a member of royalty

* a solicitor

* a life prisoner

* a respected mentor

* a favourite entertainer

*   a bishop.

And so on.

You can do this *ad infinitum*. If you like, to the 'nth' perceptual position. It's a simple, yet quick technique you can apply to a whole range of 'people problems'. It will give you a new outlook on any situation involving people.

If you, quite literally, exercise your mind in these different perspectives, it will help you to understand other people better, influence them, and achieve your goals through them in a 'win-win' fashion. It works fast.

....

You will instantly change how you feel about a person.

....

The change will take place in you – your attitude, emotions and your behaviour. This will usually affect, in turn, the other person's behaviour.

USE YOUR EMPATHY SKILLS

You can use the 'first, second and third position' process in several ways:

Solving a 'People' Problem

When facing a problem, which involves people and communication (and most problems do) deliberately envisage first and second positions and a number of third party positions. Each will provide a different angle on the nature of your problem. Think of real examples in your life. Sometimes you receive an 'insight', and often a solution emerges after a period of 'incubation'. Often the problem disappears as you see it from different points of view.

Repairing Relationships

A different perceptual perspective is
invaluable when you encounter a difficult
personal relationship. Perhaps your boss
or a colleague always rubs you up the
wrong way. By putting yourself into the
other person's shoes, you will not only
understand the person better, but you will
also change the effect they have on you.
You start to exercise emotional control
over yourself. As relationships are two-way
affairs, the other person often changes
anyway. You can 'change position' in
moments, thus immediately affecting how
you feel. Before long you will notice the
effect on the other person.

Persuading and Influencing

You will find this positioning skill
invaluable when you need to persuade,
negotiate or influence. For instance, in a
business negotiation, if you can put
yourself into the other person's emotional
shoes, you will be able to adjust your
response and method of communication
accordingly. What may be small beer to
the other party could be of significant
advantage to you. So you can often gain a
valuable negotiating edge without
conceding anything of substance. As a
bonus, in such win-win situations, you
will maintain rapport and enhance your
relationship.

GOING FOR IT

Understanding others is an emotional
competence that produces win-win
situations in selling, negotiating and
interpersonal mediation of any kind.
Along with self-understanding, it's an EQ
skill that you can apply in many areas of
your life. Practise taking positions. Start to
take a special interest in the people in
your life and notice how your own life is
enriched.

Chapter Five

Influence People

*Understanding the different needs and
desires of other people will enable
you to communicate better.*

By getting to know yourself better you
will be able to understand others
better. For instance, by getting in touch
with your own feelings, you will
appreciate other people's feelings better.
Similarly, by understanding your own
goals, desires and intentions, you will start
to take account of the very different needs
and desires of other people. That way, you
will be able to communicate better. As you

follow the easy stages in this chapter you will quickly boost your interpersonal skills.

Fortunately, we all have the innate ability to get along with people. It's not just for the chosen, personable few. In any event, interpersonal competence is an aspect of emotional intelligence that can be learnt (or, more correctly, re-learnt), improved and perfected.

People are different from one another because – just like you – they have their own desires, goals and values. Respecting these differences will not only help you to understand others better, as we saw in the previous chapter, but will help you to communicate better and thereby *influence* them for *your* purposes. This EQ skill includes creating a 'rapport' and 'getting along' with people, thereby developing worthwhile relationships. It also involves achieving 'communication outcomes'. In other words, fulfilling your own goals through other people.

GO FOR EFFECT

A communication can be described as successful if it brings about the intention you had in mind. That includes the *effect* you want to create. For example, in communicating with a person, your intention may be to:

* inform

* persuade

* frighten

* impress

* question

* motivate

*   activate

*   reassure.

And so on.

If you don't achieve the effect you wanted, then you haven't communicated effectively.

* 'He took it completely the wrong way'.

* 'I gave her the facts – I'm not responsible for her actions'.

And as it was *your* goal anyway – you are the communica*tor* – you are probably the loser, whoever was to 'blame'.

APPLY 'INTELLIGENT' GOAL CRITERIA

First decide what you want, including the *effect* you want your communication to have. This is something we don't usually think about. In this case your goal happens to be of a communication type, but you nevertheless need to apply the universal, intelligent goal-testing questions you met in Chapter 1. Let's take the first goal-testing question we met on page 20 as an example. Your communication outcome should be *specific*. Any of the following might be possibilities.

*   To persuade a person about a
    particular course of action.

*   To motivate someone to do something
    or not to do something.

*   To impress someone with a view to
    winning a sale or being offered a
    salary increase or a better job.

*   To get a useful answer that fills your
    knowledge gap.

HOW AND WHAT TO COMMUNICATE

Each of the other goal criteria you met in Chapter 1 applies equally. Once you know what you want from a communication, it will be easier to decide on how you will fulfil it. We communicate interpersonally in many different ways:

* through words

* through mannerisms

* by tone, pitch and speed of voice

* through posture, and general physiology

* through facial expressions

* with eye contact and other eye movements.

And so on.

Other than the words we choose to say or write, we adopt these behaviours unconsciously, of course.

However, interpersonal competence involves *thinking* about what and how you communicate. This especially applies when you want to prepare for an important communication such as a job interview, and when you want to improve this aspect of your EQ.

The Three Ms

There are communication factors you can consciously *pay attention to*. These could be termed 'the three Ms'. They are:

* *The medium.* Telephone, fax, e-mail, letter, newspaper, magazine, book, television, various forms of advertising and such like.

* *The message.* What should I say? What's the message I want to get across?

* *The mode, or manner.* Sometimes we need to communicate informally, such as in a passing remark or casual conversation. At other times a

communication may be more formal, such as a memo circulated to staff, a chairperson's speech, a half-yearly appraisal interview, a final interview and so on.

GETTING WHAT YOU WANT THROUGH PEOPLE

Ask yourself these sorts of questions and you can multiply the effectiveness of any communication:

* What's my **purpose**? (Check back to the 'Knowing what you want' rules in Chapter 1).

* What **effect**, or outcome do I want to achieve? – impress, warn, inform etc – see page 92? What is my true intention?

* What's the most appropriate **medium** to use, in view of my purpose?

* What **message** do I want to get across?

* What **mode** should I adopt?

These common sense questions usually produce instinctive, common sense answers. Further questions may also come to mind. Each will increase your chances of a successful communication.

A final warning letter

A formal communication, such as a final red warning reminder to pay a bill, may get no response at all. As a communication, it therefore didn't work. It was ineffective. Further formal communications may eventually,

---

perhaps through the courts, result in settlement. But this will probably entail a lot of time and expense. More to the point, it is unlikely that the *intention* was to go through the rigmarole of court proceedings. Rather, the intention was probably to get settlement as cheaply and quickly as possible. So, in this case, the communication was unsuccessful, however 'correct' the medium used, the message transmitted and the manner adopted. What different approach might the principles in this and the previous chapter suggest?

A boss's speech

In making a *formal* speech about forthcoming redundancies the managing director's intention may be to reassure staff and boost flagging morale. But if it has the reverse effect it's an ineffective communication. Conversely, an *informal* disciplinary 'chat' might be taken as victimisation, unfairness and so on. Once again, whatever its form and content, and however 'professionally' executed, the communication fails. By applying the influencing principles in this chapter, and especially considering the effect of his speech, the MD could have got a very different outcome.

MIND-TO-MIND COMMUNICATION

The bottom line is that there is no standard set of rules for communicating with people. We're all experts from about three years old anyway. If you can achieve a successful outcome, it doesn't really matter what you say or how you say it. Or, indeed, whether you use words at all.

What matters is that you transfer what is in your mind (a desire, intention – a 'communication goal', if you like) to somebody else's mind in such a way that their understanding and actions, if required, fulfil your intention. It's a *mind-to-mind* transaction. Unless there is mutual understanding, a successful outcome is unlikely.

You can create a mind-to-mind communication in three main ways:

1. Identify Interests

People who are genuinely interested in other people's hobbies, work and interests find no difficulty in creating rapport and establishing relationships. People who go out of their way to prepare for a sales meeting, interview or social gathering are usually well repaid. Even when you know a boss has to specifically do their homework to be knowledgeable about their staff, they are no less respected and admired. The critical key to winning minds is:

....

*Take an interest in other
people's interests.*

....

Whether you have to work at this or it
comes naturally, a genuine interest in
other people is a characteristic of a well-
developed emotional intelligence.

2. Align Goals, Needs and Desires

Identify common objectives. If both
parties want to

* 'bring this to a successful conclusion,
  one way or another'

* do a deal

* sign a contract

* or agree on a course of action

they will tend to co-operate in that mutual
objective. There will be a 'meeting of
minds'. This applies in even the most
troublesome kinds of communication,
such as pay negotiations between

management and unions, and legal disputes such as in divorce proceedings. Decisions over custody of children illustrate the importance of common objectives, when the best interests of the children are the overriding, common priority. A shared outcome avoids many a communication pitfall.

So the quick fix rule is simple:

....

You know what you want.
Try to establish what the other
person wants.

....

Identify this up front. It will help if you
see from different positions as you learnt
in Chapter 4.

3. Share Values and Beliefs

A person may belong to the same
profession, have the same hobby, hail
from the same hometown, and suchlike,
but if they do not share the other person's
values – what is important in life – any
communication will be doomed to fail.
For instance, do you really want to work
for an employer, or have as a partner
someone whose basic values are very
different to your own?

A person with a high EQ tends to sort out these personal issues. They will be less likely to land up in wrong relationships, or get involved in no-win communications. So if you can *agree on what is important*, you are well on the way to a successful communication outcome.

GOING FOR IT

When it comes to influencing people, it doesn't matter whether you are a 'people person', an introvert or an extrovert. You can increase your interpersonal intelligence by applying these simple principles. You can go on to develop these interpersonal skills to any level you wish. But by applying the simple EQ know-how in this chapter you will start to see changes straight away.

Chapter Six

Deal With Conflict

*Bridging the communication gap
becomes the 'communication outcome'.*

D epending on your point of view,
many communication outcomes
involve conflict of various kinds. At one
extreme you have the handling 'difficult
people' kind of communication. At the
other end, you have all sorts of one-on-
one interview, selling or negotiation
situations where some difference between
the parties has to be reconciled.

You learnt in Chapters 4 and 5 about understanding other people and communicating effectively. These simple principles apply in any interpersonal communication.

BRIDGING THE COMMUNICATION GAP

The 'conflict' is the gap between what's in one person's mind and what is in another's. That 'gap' might be between:

* The price a seller wants and what the buyer is willing to pay.

* The salary an employer thinks an employee is worth and what the employee thinks.

* Behaviour which one person thinks is normal or commendable and which another person takes exception to.

*   The demands of an irate customer and
     what the company is willing to
     concede to give satisfaction.

Bridging the communication gap becomes
the 'communication outcome'. Otherwise,
dealing with conflict follows the same
communication principles. Nor does it
demand special people skills. It's just
another way of looking at a goal that
involves communicating with people.

MATCHING

The principles and techniques you will
learn in this chapter come under the
general term of 'matching'. They apply in
any interpersonal situation, and
complement what you have learnt so far.
They apply equally in the most extreme
cases of dealing with difficult people. So
the know-how you will gain will give you
confidence in the great majority of more
'ordinary' people problems you will face.
More positively, these powerful techniques
will significantly increase your
interpersonal intelligence, which you can
apply in other ways.

Matching means being perceived to be 'like' the person you are communicating with. It takes many forms. For instance, you can match a person's:

* posture and general physiology

* tone, speed and pitch of your voice

* mannerisms, such as hand movements

* facial expressions that can clearly show how you feel

* eye contact and other eye movements

* interests, such as a hobby or sport

* goals and objectives

* values and beliefs.

Matching usually happens unconsciously. However, matching skills can be improved by conscious ('intelligent') application, training and practice.

Some books tell you to keep cool and speak in a steady quiet tone of voice when dealing with an angry, over-emotional person. In most people's experience, however, this doesn't work. In fact, the cooler and calmer a colleague or partner remains, when the other person is ready to explode, the more animosity is fuelled. Such a 'controlled' attitude is more likely to be interpreted as 'cold', 'insensitive', 'uncaring' or 'inhuman'.

On the other hand, a skilled customer service manager will soon gain rapport with the angriest customer against the common enemy of the company's rules or incompetent staff. It is 'matching' that usually turns out to be the secret of their success. In fact, matching has been shown to be a universal feature of good communication.

Match Posture and General Physiology

Watch two people in deep conversation and notice how each person's posture tends to mirror the other person. Both may be leaning back, for instance, with hands clasped behind their heads and legs crossed. Or, when facing each other across a table, leaning forward with open hands. We do this unconsciously all the time.

Whatever the *content* of the communication, the matched posture and general demeanour is a good sign that people are 'on the same wavelength' or in 'rapport'. 'Matching', or 'mirroring' behaviour is typical of a person with high

emotional intelligence and 'people skills'.
However, it is something we can all do,
and quickly see the results in
communication successes.

Match Voice Tone, Pitch and Speed

We likewise usually match our voices unknowingly. For instance, both parties tend to adjust the speed, tone and pitch of their voice towards that of the other person. This is especially noticeable when we address very young children or old people.

The 'communication' might be an animated recounting of a good story, delivering welcome news, or the slow discussion of a mutually sad occurrence. In each case matching indicates rapport, 'coming together' and the 'meeting of minds'. Conversely, a voice mismatch usually spells a lost sale, unsuccessful interview or angrier customer. In short, an ineffective communication.

Matching voice characteristics is an important aspect of interpersonal competence. Top salespeople and counsellors often exhibit this natural skill. However, we can all consciously apply these simple techniques and see the results in transformed communication skills and relationships.

Match Expressions and Mannerisms

A number of common facial expressions
have been identified that cover basic
emotions, like surprise, disgust, disbelief
etc. These are universal and have been
shown to apply in widely different
cultures. In fact, each of these broad
emotional types involves an infinite
variety of sub-meanings. Each nuance of
facial expression requires hundreds of
facial muscles, choreographed in a
moment-by-moment dance of emotion.
From childhood, we have been able to
read these expressions and mannerisms.
Having such communicative power, such
skills are worth *re-learning*.

Contrary to what might have been expected, people are rarely conscious of matching behaviour, even when it is done purposely in this way. We are more concerned with the *content* of a communication. So you needn't feel self-conscious or 'manipulative'. Matching is a feature of rapport in all person-to-person communication, but there is always room for improvement.

GOING FOR IT

These effective, win-win communication skills are examples of interpersonal intelligence. Try out matching at the first opportunity, and notice the effect, especially when handling conflict.

Deal With Conflict

Chapter Seven

Get Motivated

*Self-motivation is an important
feature of EQ.*

Self-motivation is an emotional *resource* of the sort you met in Chapter 3. As emotional *currency* it is very useful, and like money *exchangeable* for all sorts of things.

For example, if you are motivated to do something:

*   You will overcome the common 'not enough time' problem.

* You will not give up part way through.

* You will not depend too much on others to achieve your goals.

* You will get pleasure in the process of reaching a goal – in the journey as well as the destination.

* You will get things done – make things happen.

* You will motivate others around you.

* Life will seem worthwhile.

CALL ON INNER RESOURCES

Fortunately we are all motivated by something. We each have 'emotional hotspots' that seem to propel us to achieve things. These may be limited to a part of our lives – such as a hobby or special interest, or a part of our work we really enjoy.

You can call on motivating resources whenever you need them. By recalling the feelings of a positive, successful memory, you can bring them into service to help achieve your present goal. Motivation, like any emotion, is transferable. And often all you need is the right frame of mind to *get started* on a not-too-appealing task. A little bit of self-motivation, at the right time, can tip the balance between success and failure.

The more you call upon positive, empowering memories, the more quickly and effectively you will be able to bring the best state of mind to whatever you want to achieve. It just takes a moment. With practice it will become a powerful emotional skill that will change your whole approach to whatever you undertake. Like any habit, mental or physical, you soon get to do this without thinking.

FOCUS ON WHAT YOU WANT

The goal-setting exercises in Chapter 1
enabled you to focus on what you want.
That meant being specific, and clearly
visualising completed goals as strong,
inner targets. The more realistic and
compelling your inner target, the more
you will be motivated to achieve it. Apply
this to each of the goals you listed and
notice how your motivation increases as
you value the end target more highly. It's
the natural way of human achievement.

Visualising success is not just a quick-fix motivator. It can be a pleasurable part of the ongoing process of achievement. You *pre-experience* your goal, in multi-sensory mode – sights, sounds, and feelings. You get the pleasure (including the desired state of mind) inherent in your goal. Then, in a self-fulfilling way, you realise your inner goal-picture. That's the stuff of a million human dreams.

CREATE A MOTIVATING CHALLENGE

One of the goal questions you met in Chapter 1 was 'Is my goal at the right level'. By adjusting the size or complexity of a goal, you can make it motivating. Not so small that you can't bring yourself to start, and not so big that you unconsciously act as if it wasn't there. A deadline, even a self-set, or contrived one, for instance, can do wonders for your motivation.

Go back to your goals and give them a motivation score of 1 to 10. Then break some down into more manageable parts, or give yourself tighter timescales and

notice how your motivation ratings
quickly change. You can make big, quick-
fix changes instantly just by carrying out
the process. Even minor goal adjustments
can rocket your motivation, and chances
of final success.

REWARD YOURSELF

Often the problem is not how to get *started*, but how to *keep going*, especially when things are going the wrong way. Or properly finishing a job when the interesting, challenging part is over. This is when you have to contrive self-motivation by mini, 'stepping-stone' goals and self-rewards. The first draft of a report, for instance, a chapter of a book, getting building plans accepted, succeeding at an initial interview, making a telephone call for information – each is a stepping-stone towards a bigger goal.

Build in motivation by giving yourself little rewards to look forward to. A coffee when you have completed your present task, or a five-minute walk round the park might be all that is needed. Or a meal out with your other half if you can meet a more important, interim target by the weekend.

Get to know the specific rewards you respond to ('one man's reward . . .'). Check back on 'understanding yourself' in Chapter 2, and in particular what you value most. Don't be too generous, or too hard on yourself. Self-motivation requires emotional intelligence, but:

....

You can quickly learn it by doing it, and get better by doing it more.

....

Picture each goal-success, using your childhood imagination. You can reward yourself as frequently and appropriately as you need to to get things done.

GOING FOR IT

Self-motivation is one of the foundations of intrapersonal intelligence. It can mean the difference between extraordinary human achievement and mediocrity. You learnt how to tap emotional memory-resources and manage you moods in Chapter 3. Motivation is a mood worth harnessing and is one of the keys to emotional intelligence.

149

Chapter Eight

Think Straight

Quality thinking incorporates left and right brain processes in an awesome goal-achieving duo.

IQ-type thinking is rational and logical. It is also *conscious* thinking. So it's the only kind of thinking we usually think about. In fact we can only think of half a dozen things consciously at one time, so this part of our thinking represents just the tip of the mental iceberg.

Some thinking happens in a completely non-logical way. The right brain works

holistically, and can jump to solutions
('insights', 'Eureka's', 'brainwaves')
without our knowing the intermediate
logical steps. More 'thinking' happens
while we are asleep in REM (rapid eye
movement) mode. This seems to be the
sorting out phase for the billions of
sensations we cope with in a waking day.
In fact, 'sleeping on a problem', we know,
can produce quality thought when
conscious, grinding mental effort fails. All
kinds of habitual behaviour, such as riding
a bike or drinking soup, is unconsciously
choreographed in our brain.

GENES AND GENIUS

Emotional intelligence embraces all that.
It's not confined to cerebral, logical
thought. In particular, it majors in
intrapersonal intelligence (understanding
yourself – including your emotions) and
interpersonal intelligence (understanding
and relating to others). So quality
thinking incorporates left and right brain
processes in an awesome goal-achieving
duo. It's this holistic-yet-analytical, big
picture-detail thinking that translates into
the human achievement we associate with
genius, accomplishment, purpose and
'getting things done'.

As we have seen, developing your EQ can be done quickly and continuously, in easy, manageable chunks. Unlike, IQ (so we are told), it doesn't seem to depend on heredity, nor on language and other culturally-dependant learning. In some cases, however, you will need a new outlook. In particular a belief in your inherent ability and potential as a person.

···

Opening your mind to what you are capable of may demand a change of lifestyle.

···

As we saw, you may need to pursue 'being' rather than 'having' and 'getting' goals (see page 15). Or you may need to make time for insights and creativity to bubble up to your conscious mind. More than anything, you need to be open to change.

Fortunately there are things you can do to create a new perspective and make fuller use of your experience, innate intelligence and emotional resources.

Here's how you can begin to think straight and start to accomplish things you could not have imagined:

1. When Overloaded with Information

* Walk away.

* Close up the files.

* Tackle another task with a fresh mind.

* Put the present job out of your mind until tomorrow, then see things in a fresh light.

* Ask yourself: 'What are the top three facts concerning my problem or situation' – and don't waste time on the others.

2. When You Don't Have Enough Information

* Mentally review everything you *do* know, decide what you *don't* know, then put the matter out of your mind.

* Expect ideas to come to you when least expected.

* Think about who you may be able to get help from, and ask them.

* Ask yourself what information you would like to have if you could get it.

* Remind yourself of exactly what you want, and vividly imagine having fully achieved it.

3. When in a Crisis

* Take a few minutes away from the eye of the storm.

* Sleep on it. Most 'crises' have been building up for a long time, and you can usually survive until bedtime.

* Think about the good things in your life so you keep things in context.

* Trust your amazing brain that has got you out of similar situations in the past.

4. When in Two Minds

* Relax and let your mind 'freewheel'.

* Think about what feels right.

* Toss a coin, agreeing first which alternative action heads and tails will represent. If you feel like tossing it again, choose the other way (your unconscious mind is saying 'no'). If you are happy with how the coin falls, follow that course of action.

WHAT TO THINK ABOUT

Thinking doesn't change the world. But it's where change starts. Think about:

*   Your purposes – what you really want. Apply the goal criteria in Chapter 1.

*   Each *completed* goal, in vivid, realistic, multi-sensory mode.

*   Yourself. Your values. What is important to you. Do the 'values' exercise in Chapter 2.

*   Other people. Check back on the three basic perceptual positions in Chapter 4.

GOING FOR IT

We use just a fraction of our potential brainpower (and that includes the Einsteins of the world). So we are all capable of extraordinary levels of improvement in the quality and effectiveness of our thinking. Be prepared to translate your thoughts into behaviour and achievement. That's what marks out emotionally intelligent people like you.

Chapter Nine

Make Things Happen

*IQ is more about knowing,
while EQ is more about doing.*

People with high emotional
intelligence tend to get things done,
make things happen, and have an effect
on their world.

This takes the form of goal-orientation, and the sort of skills you met in Chapter 1. It demands clear values and purpose (Chapter 2), which are the foundation for making decisions and single-minded action. It also calls upon the emotional control you learnt about in Chapter 3. EQ comes into its own when you 'couldn't be bothered', couldn't keep your attention, or just 'didn't get round to doing it'. It translates dreams, ideas and goals into reality.

....

EQ makes things happen.

....

Some people are natural, 'up front', action-oriented 'doers'. Others spend time reflecting, analysing and deciding. But, as we have seen, these EQ characteristics are learnable and doable. Anyone can make a goal list and apply the criteria. Anyone can recall an empowering, motivating memory and face a present task in a better state of mind.

THE FOUR-STAGE SUCCESS MODEL

Making things happen follows a simple, four-stage model that you can apply to any kind of goal:

1. Decide what you want.

2. Do something.

3. Notice what happens.

4. Change what you do until you get your desired outcome.

Stop Trying

High IQ people, when they don't achieve a goal, often become more focused, redouble their effort, re-analyse the situation and generally try harder. On the face of it, this is an intelligent approach. High-EQ people, on the other hand, take a more pragmatic approach to 'failure'. To them, it's just information – feedback. You learn that if you do certain things then

certain things happen. It follows that if you do something different you will get a different outcome. You can put it this way:

···

If you always do what you always did you'll always get what you always got.

···

In this light, the 'try, try and try (the same thing) again' approach is not very clever. Better to try something different and notice what happens. Stop trying too hard. Let your brain take the strain.

Make Meaningful Mistakes

Emotionally intelligent people can live
with mistakes and failures – although they
don't seem to view them as such. They
make far more 'mistakes' than high-IQ
people (or at least are more ready to
admit them). But, conversely, they achieve
much more. In fact, they attempt much
more. They make things happen. They
have fewer inhibitions about 'trial and
error' methods and 'having a go'. They
seem to cope with uncertainty and change.

172

As a result (like children before inhibitions set in), they tend to learn very quickly. Excelling as they do in people skills, they have learnt to accept all manner of human failings, and to live with unpredictability and continuous change.

The four-stage success model, which anyone can apply to his or her life, reflects this highly effective, emotionally intelligent goal-achieving approach. As you think back to successes in the past, you will probably notice that you adopted this flexible, goal-oriented approach. By applying the model *consciously* to the less successful areas of your life, you will enjoy similar success. It's the way human beings have got to where they are.

GOING FOR IT

Like the goal-setting process you learnt in Chapter 1, this four-stage process will become a habit. Habitual achievement – making things happen – marks out the person of superior emotional intelligence. As we have seen, this is less to do with genes than common sense application, know-how and the kind of self-knowledge we can all acquire if we care to.

Chapter Ten

Get On In Life

*Learn 'habits of success' according to
your criteria for success.*

Improving your EQ can happen in
frequent small steps, as you create
realistic, manageable goals, understand
yourself and your values and attitudes
better, and take control of moment-by-
moment emotions. As with any repeated
thought process or activity, we create
habits. Using your intelligence in the way
you have learnt, this means 'habits of
success' according to your own criteria for
success. Or, the ability to get on in life.

As we saw right at the beginning, in setting your goals you identify things you want to know, have or get, and do. However, reflecting on these goals, it often turns out that they are stepping-stone goals you hope will take you toward bigger, longer-term *being* goals. These are the sorts of goals associated with 'fulfilment', 'purpose', and 'getting on' in life.

GOING FOR 'BEING' GOALS

For instance:

* If I get that, I will *be* content.

* If I can only do that, I will *be* happy.

* If I knew that, I would *be* more secure.

However, we have all met people who seem to be happier than us without the possessions and trappings of success. They seem to enjoy what they have got, take pleasure in the present, and live life to the full. They have somehow learnt how to 'be content', to 'be happy' and to succeed according to their own, inner yardstick of success.

Once you learn how to achieve these
higher, *being* goals, you can bypass many
of the interim goals upon which you
thought success depended. You can go
straight to your important goals in the
quickest, most direct, most resourceful,
most *intelligent* way. Specifically, that
means going for the end *state* you learnt
about in Chapter 3.

This special skill is part of your goal
achieving know-how. By lifting your sights
to *being* goals, you will direct your EQ
towards meaningful life-important goals.
Being goals follow the same goal-testing
criteria you met in Chapter 1. So there's
no mystique about getting where you
ultimately want to be.

Emotional intelligence draws upon your whole, unique mind-body resources. It requires a purpose. You are not an automaton. Intelligence is not just cerebral, but incorporates your every emotion and the unconscious part of your mind, which is as fathomless as the ocean depths. If you haven't identified such a life purpose it's never too late. You can do this quickly and easily by following the goals and value processes you learnt in Chapters 1 and 2.

EQ is good news for most of us who were not over gifted at birth and have had to cope with a few intellectual blind spots. You can:

*   *learn* it

*   *do* it

*   continuously *improve* it

*   *apply* it in just about any part of your life.

And that with hardly an intelligence gene in sight. And it cannot exist in a vacuum. It's social savvy. It affects how you communicate with and relate to other people as much as it concerns you as a person. Most importantly, your boosted EQ can have an immediate effect on your life.

EQ AND PERSONAL SUCCESS

EQ has a lot going for it. For one, it's a moveable feast, and you can improve it in the ways you have learnt in this book. So, whatever your 'intelligence', you are not stuck with it. Better still, EQ is the kind of intelligence that copes best in our modern, changing world, where people skills, and self-management, rather than academic attainment, are the currency of success.

EQ takes the barriers away from personal success, in any field. The limit is your brain potential – which isn't a limit at all. It doesn't matter what you may have been conditioned to believe about your ability and lot in life. It may not be true that anything is possible, but it's an intelligent presupposition if you want to live up to your full potential as a person. Confidence in your self and your potential is a big factor in achievement – and it's smart.

Think about:

* What intelligence means to you and the people in your life – those who might influence your 'success' and future.

* What you want to do or be through improving your emotional intelligence – what is your purpose.

* What are some aspects of intelligence you've met in this book that you particularly value, and want to learn and develop more.

* How you might behave differently given your new, self-knowledge and interpersonal know-how.

* How committed you are to living up to the full potential of your intelligence, and getting out of life what you know you are capable of.

GOING FOR IT

By tapping your innate intelligence you get to know some truly *intelligent* things:

* What you really want.

* What is important to you.

* How to manage your moods, and unlock unlimited emotional resources.

* How you can habitually achieve what you set out to achieve.

You are what you think and feel. And you can think and feel what you decide to. That's being emotionally intelligent. That's what you were born to be.

Notes

....

....

....

....

....

....

....

....

....

....

Notes

....

....

....

....

....

....

....

....

....

....

....

....

Notes

....

....

....

....

....

....

....

....

....

....

....

....

Other Books by Harry Alder

The Right Brain Manager (Piatkus)

NLP: The New Art and Science of Getting What You Want
(Piatkus)

NLP in 21 Days (Piatkus)

NLP for Trainers (McGraw Hill)

NLP for Managers (Piatkus)

The Right Brain Time Manager (Piatkus)

The Ultimate How To Book (Gower)

Mind to Mind Marketing (Kogan Page)

Think Like a Leader (Piatkus)

Remembering Names and Faces (How To Books)

How To Live Longer (How To Books)

Masterstroke (Piatkus)

Train Your Brain (Piatkus)

Corporate Charisma (Piatkus)